Martial Arts

Written by Eamonn O'Farrell

Contents

Tricky words to practise before reading this book:

martial, colour

What are Martial Arts?

Martial arts are a kind of sport.
Lots of people learn martial arts.

There are different kinds of martial arts.
Can you name one?

Clothes

You need these clothes
for martial arts.
There are different belts.
The colour of the belt shows
how good you are.

beginner

belt

expert

Respect

Respect is important in martial arts.
You bow to show your respect.

Standing

There are lots of ways to stand in martial arts.

How you stand is called your **stance**.

Ready stance

Put fists together.

Stand with feet apart.

Forward stance

Put fists at
your sides.

Bend this leg

Keep back leg
straight.

Horseriding stance

Put one fist forward.

Put one fist at the side.

Bend both legs.

Tiger stance

Put fists forward.

Bend this leg.

Keep back leg straight.

q

Fitness

Martial arts can make you fit and strong.

They can help your speed and **flexibility**.

Practising

It takes a long time to be good at martial arts.

It is important to learn properly.
No one will get hurt that way.

You can do martial arts on your own
or with someone.

If you keep learning martial arts, one day you could do this!

Glossary

flexibility   bend the body in different ways

respect   treating people well

stance   way of standing